Stan's Glittering Trail

Written by
Cath Jones

Illustrated by
Brian Fitzgerald

Stan sat next to Slug in the moonlight.

"Look at the moon and the stars glittering up there!" said Stan.
"I am just a dull, brown snail.
I wish I was glittering too."

Stan felt a little sad.

"If I can get as high as the moon and stars," said Stan, "do you think I will glitter too?"

"Stan, you are such a foolish snail! You cannot get as high as the moon," said Slug.

"Look at that frog jump," said Stan. "How high do you think she can jump?"

Stan got some frogs and set up a frog stack. Then he sat on it!

The frogs sprang up and Stan went with them!

BOING! BOING! BOING!

"Yippee!" said Stan.

But Stan and the frogs did not get as high as the moon.

Stan felt a little sad.

"Is that a kangaroo hopping down the track? Come on, Slug. Be quick! She will get me to the moon," said Stan.

Get set, GO!

The kangaroo sprang up and Stan went with her!

BOING! BOING! BOING!

"Yippee!" said Stan.

But Stan and the kangaroo did not get as high as the moon.

Stan felt a little sad.

"Look at that little owl sitting in the tree," said Stan. "He will get me to the moon!"

Stan slid onto the back of the owl.

Squelch, squelch, squelch.

When the owl shot into the air, Stan felt no fear!

ZOO-OO-OO-M!

They shot higher and higher and higher.

"I did it," Stan said. "I got as high as the moon! Look up there, at my glittering trail."